Sufi Prayers

Sufi Prayers

The Prayers, Worship, and Remembrances of the Inayati Sufis

Gender Inclusive Edition
Adapted into Modern English

Hazrat
Pir-o-Murshid
Inayat Khan

Edited and Annotated by
Pir Netanel Miles-Yépez

Albion
Andalus
Boulder, Colorado
2015

"The old shall be renewed,

and the new shall be made holy."
— Rabbi Avraham Yitzhak Kook

Albion-Andalus, Inc.
P. O. Box 19852
Boulder, CO 80308
www.albionandalus.com

Cover design by Daryl McCool
Design and layout by Albion-Andalus Books
"Rose-Heart and Wings" illustration
© 2008 Netanel Miles-Yépez

Manufactured in the United States of America

ISBN-13: 978-0692568712 (Albion-Andalus Books)
ISBN-10: 0692568719

CONTENTS

Editor's Preface

In this edition of the Universalist Sufi prayers, worship service, and remembrances of Hazrat Inayat Khan, I have edited and adapted the originals for clarity in modern English and made them gender inclusive (rather than using the masculine personal pronoun in an inclusive sense, as was the convention in Pir-o-Murshid's day). I have also added notes where I thought it necessary to explain the context, non-English vocabulary, or the origins of various prayers. It should be remembered that the versions of the prayers and remembrances in this booklet are interpretations of the originals and open to error. I take full responsibility for any such errors I have introduced. Please know that I have approached the material with the utmost respect and have only made changes to them in the hope that the updated language and gender inclusivity will help to spread the Message of God "far and wide." I encourage any readers who are new to them to acquaint themselves with the originals (which may be obtained from the various Inayati organizations) and learn the differences. It goes without saying that one should learn to recite the prayers in accordance with the custom of one's own community. These versions are only to give you options for use in your personal practice.

Pir Netanel Mu'in ad-Din, Boulder, Colorado,
dedicated to my most beloved friend, Alia,
November 4th, 2015, the day on which we read . . .

By the power of prayer,
we open the door of the heart,
in which God, the ever-forgiving,
the all merciful, abides.

Sufi Prayers

The Prayers, Worship,
and Remembrances
of the Inayati Sufis

MORNING PRAYERS

Invocation

*Raise your gaze to the sky,
then drop your chin to your
chest, as you say:*

This is not my body;

*Turn the chin toward
the left shoulder, then allow
it to travel across the torso
to the right shoulder,
while you say:*

This is the temple
Of the heart.

Toward the One

Toward the One,
The Perfection of Love,
Harmony, and Beauty,
The Only Being,
United with all
The Illuminated Souls,
Who form the
Embodiment
Of the Master,
The Spirit of Guidance.

Saum

Praise be to You,
God, Most High,
Omnipotent,
Omnipresent,
All-Pervading,
The Only Being.

Take us in Your
Parental arms,
Raise us from the
Denseness of the Earth!

Your beauty
We do worship;
To You we
Willingly surrender.

Merciful and
Compassionate God,
Ideal Sustainer
Of Humanity,
You only
Do we worship,
And toward You alone
Do we aspire!

Open our hearts
Toward Your Beauty;
Illuminate our souls
With Divine Light.

O Perfection of Love,
Harmony and Beauty,
All-powerful Creator,
Sustainer, Judge,
And Forgiver of
Our shortcomings,
Sovereign God
Of the East
And of the West,
Of the Worlds
Above and below,
Of the seen
And unseen beings,
Pour upon us Your
Love and Your Light!

Give sustenance
To our bodies,
Hearts, and souls;
Use us for the purpose
That Your
Wisdom chooses;
Guide us on the path
Of Your Own Goodness!

Draw us closer to You
In every moment
Of our lives,
Until in us is reflected
Your Grace, Your Glory,
Your Wisdom, Your Joy
And Your Peace!
Amin.

REMEMBRANCE

*Recite the next line
eleven times:*

Pour upon us Your
Love and Your Light!

PIR

Inspirer of my mind,
Consoler of my heart,
Healer of my spirit,
Your Presence lifts me
From Earth unto Heaven!

Your words flow
As the sacred river;
Your thought rises
As a Divine spring,
Your tenderness awakens
Sympathy in my heart!

Beloved Teacher,
Your very being
Is forgiveness.

The clouds of
Doubt and fear
Are scattered by your
Piercing glance.

All ignorance vanishes
In your illuminating
Presence.

A new hope
Is born in my heart
As I breathe Your
Peaceful atmosphere!

Inspiring Guide
Through life's
Labyrinthine ways,
In you, I feel
An abundance
Of blessing!
Amin.

Silsila

*Hazrat Muhammad,
Rasul Allah*

Hazrat 'Ali, Wali Allah

*Hazrat Khwaja
Hasan Basri*

*Hazrat Khwaja 'Abd
al-Wahid bin Zayd*

*Hazrat Khwaja Fuzayl
bin 'Ayaz*

*Hazrat Khwaja Ibrahim
ibn Adham Balkhi*

*Hazrat Khwaja
Huzayfa Mar'ishi*

*Hazrat Khwaja
Hubayra Basri*

*Hazrat Khwaja Mumshad
'Ulu Dinwari*

*Hazrat Khwaja Abu Ishaq
Shami Chishti*

Hazrat Khwaja Abu Ahmad
Abdal Chishti

Hazrat Khwaja Abu
Muhammad Chishti

Hazrat Khwaja Nasir ad-Din
Abu Yusuf Chishti

Hazrat Khwaja Qutb ad-Din
Mawdud Chishti

Hazrat Khwaja
Hajji Sharif Zindani

Hazrat Khwaja
'Usman Harvani

Hazrat Khwaja Mu'in ad-Din
Hasan Sanjari-Ajmiri

Hazrat Khwaja Qutb ad-Din
Mas'ud, Bakhtiyar Kaki

Hazrat Khwaja Farid ad-Din
Mas'ud, Ganj-i Shakar,
Ajhodani

Hazrat Khwaja
Nizam ad-Din Mahbub-i
Ilahi, Badauni

Hazrat Khwaja Nasir ad-Din
Mahmud, Chiragh Dihlavi

Hazrat Sheikh al-Masheikh
Kamal ad-Din 'Allama

Hazrat Sheikh al-Masheikh
Siraj ad-Din

Hazrat Sheikh al-Masheikh
Ilm ad-Din

Hazrat Sheikh al-Masheikh
Mahmud Rajan

Hazrat Sheikh al-Masheikh
Jamal ad-Din Jamman

Hazrat Sheikh al-Masheikh
Hasan Muhammad

Hazrat Sheikh al-Masheikh
Muhammad A'zam

Hazrat Sheikh al-Masheikh
Yahya Madani

Hazrat Sheikh al-Masheikh
Shah Kalim Allah
Jahanabadi

UNIVERSEL

O Maker, Molder,
And Builder of
The Universe,
Build with Your
Own hands
The Universel,
Our Temple for
Your Divine Message
Of Love, Harmony,
And Beauty.
Amin.

*Hazrat Sheikh al-Masheikh
Nizam ad-Din Awrangabadi*

*Hazrat Sheikh al-Masheikh
Mawlana Fakhr ad-Din*

*Hazrat Sheikh al-Masheikh
Ghulam Qutb ad-Din*

*Hazrat Sheikh al-Masheikh
Nasir ad-Din Mahmud,
Kali-Shah*

*Hazrat Sheikh al-Masheikh
Muhammad Hasan
Jili Kalimi*

*Hazrat Sheikh al-Masheikh
Muhammad Abu Hashim
Madani*

*Hazrat Pir-o-Murshid
'Inayat Khan*

DEDICATION

*Raise your gaze to the sky,
then drop your chin to your
chest, as you say:*

This is not my body;

*Turn the chin toward
the left shoulder, then allow
it to travel across the torso
to the right shoulder,
while you say:*

This is the temple of God.

MID-DAY PRAYERS

INVOCATION

*Raise your gaze to the sky,
then drop your chin to your
chest, as you say:*

This is not my body;

*Turn the chin toward
the left shoulder, then allow
it to travel across the torso
to the right shoulder,
while you say:*

This is the temple
Of the heart.

TOWARD THE ONE

Toward the One,
The Perfection of Love,
Harmony, and Beauty,
The Only Being,
United with all
The Illuminated Souls,
Who form the
Embodiment
Of the Master,
The Spirit of Guidance.

SALAT

Our most
Gracious Sustainer,
Anointing Savior
Of Humanity,
We greet You
With all humility;
You are the First Cause
And the Last Effect,
The Divine Light
And the Spirit of
Guidance,
Alpha and Omega!

Your Light is in all Forms,
Your Love in all Beings:

*Take a moment to imagine
how this is so, as Murshid
suggests . . .*

In a loving mother,
In a kind father,
In an innocent child,
In a helpful friend,
In an inspiring teacher.

*Nor should you limit yourself
to these examples in your
personal prayer.*

Allow us to
Recognize You
In all Your holy
Names and Forms:

*Think of the various
"Names and Forms" by
which God is known in
different religions, and even
as embodied in the various
Messengers of those religions
throughout history. These
are some that Murshid
suggests . . .*

As Rama, as Krishna,
As Shiva, as Buddha;
Let us know You as
Abraham, as Solomon,
As Zarathustra, as Moses,
As Jesus, as Muhammad

*If you wish, you may add
others in your personal
prayer.*

And in many other
Names and forms
Known and unknown
To the world!

We adore Your past;
Your Presence deeply
Enlightens our being;
And we look for
Your blessing
In the future!

O Messenger of God!
You, Whose heart
Constantly
Reaches upward,
You come to Earth
With a Message,
As a dove descending
From above
When religion decays,
Speaking the Word
That fills Your mouth,
As light fills the
Crescent Moon.

Let the Star
Of the Divine Light
Shining in Your heart
Be reflected in the hearts
Of Your devotees!

May the Message of God
Reach far and wide!

Illuminating
And making
The whole of Humanity
Into a single Family
In the Parenthood of God!
Amin.

REMEMBRANCE

*Recite the next line
eleven times:*

May the Message of God
Reach far and wide!

NABI

A torch in the
Darkness,
A staff during
My weakness,
A rock in the
Weariness of life,
You, my masterful guide,
Make Earth a paradise!

Your thought gives me
An ethereal joy;
Your light illuminates
My life's path,
Your words inspire me
With Divine Wisdom;
I follow in your footsteps,
Which lead me
To the eternal goal!

Comforter of the
Broken-hearted,
Support of those
In need,
Friend of the
Lovers of Truth,
Blessed and
Masterful guide,
You are the
Prophet of God!
Amin.

UNIVERSEL

O Maker, Molder,
And Builder of
The Universe,
Build with Your
Own hands
The Universel,
Our Temple for
Your Divine Message
Of Love, Harmony,
And Beauty.
Amin.

DEDICATION

*Raise your gaze to the sky,
then drop your chin to your
chest, as you say:*

This is not my body;

*Turn the chin toward
the left shoulder, then allow
it to travel across the torso
to the right shoulder,
while you say:*

This is the temple of God.

EVENING PRAYERS

INVOCATION

Raise your gaze to the sky,
then drop your chin to your
chest, as you say:

This is not my body;

Turn the chin toward
the left shoulder, then allow
it to travel across the torso
to the right shoulder,
while you say:

This is the temple
Of the heart.

TOWARD THE ONE

Toward the One,
The Perfection of Love,
Harmony, and Beauty,
The Only Being,
United with all
The Illuminated Souls,
Who form the
Embodiment
Of the Master,
The Spirit of Guidance.

KHATUM

O Perfection of Love,
Harmony, and Beauty,
Sustainer of Heaven
And Earth,
Open our hearts
That we may hear
Your Voice,
Constantly coming
From within.

Disclose to us
Your Divine Light,
Hidden in our souls,
That we may know
And understand life
better.

Merciful and
Compassionate God,
Give us Your great
Goodness;
Teach us Your loving
Forgiveness;
Raise us above
The distinctions
And differences
That divide us.

Send us the Peace
Of Your Divine Spirit,
And unite us all
In Your Perfect Being.
Amin.

REMEMBRANCE

*Recite the next line
eleven times:*

Disclose to us
Your Divine Light!

RASUL

Warner of
Coming dangers,
Awakener of the
World from sleep,
Deliverer of the
Message of God,
You are our Savior.

The Sun at the
Dawn of Creation,
The light of the
Whole Universe,
The fulfillment of
God's purpose,
You, the life Eternal,
We seek refuge
In your loving
Embrace.

Spirit of Guidance,
Source of all Beauty,
Creator of Harmony,
Love, Lover,
And Beloved Sustainer,
You are our Divine Ideal.
Amin.

UNIVERSEL

O Maker, Molder,
And Builder of
The Universe,
Build with Your
Own hands
The Universel,
Our Temple for
Your Divine Message
Of Love, Harmony,
And Beauty.
Amin.

DEDICATION

*Raise your gaze to the sky,
then drop your chin to your
chest, as you say:*

This is not my body;

*Turn the chin toward
the left shoulder, then allow
it to travel across the torso
to the right shoulder, while
you say:*

This is the temple of God.

OCCASIONAL PRAYERS

BLESSING

May the blessings of God
Rest upon you;
May God's peace
Abide with you;
May God's Presence
Illuminate your hearts,
Now and forevermore.
Amin.

DU'A

Save me,
My Sustainer,
From the earthly passions
And attachments
That blind Humanity!

Save me,
My Sustainer,
From the temptations
Of power, fame
And wealth
That keep us from
Your Glorious Vision!

Save me,
My Sustainer,
From the souls
Constantly occupied
With hurting and
Harming others,
Who take pleasure
In another's pain!

Save me,
My Sustainer,
From the evil eye
Of envy and jealousy
That falls upon
Your bountiful gifts!

Save me,
My Sustainer,
From falling
Into the hands
Of the Earth's
Playful children,
Lest they use me
In their games,
And break me
In their ends!

Save me,
My Sustainer,
From all manner
Of injury
Coming from
The bitterness
Of my adversaries,
And from the ignorance
Of my loving friends!
Amin.

PRAYER FOR PEACE

Send Your Peace,
My Sustainer,
Which is perfect
And everlasting,
That our souls
May radiate peace.

Send Your Peace,
My Sustainer,
That we may think,
Act and speak
Harmoniously.

Send Your Peace,
My Sustainer,
That we may be
Contented
And grateful for
Your bountiful gifts.

Send Your Peace,
My Sustainer,
That amidst our
Worldly strife
We may enjoy
Your bliss.

Send Your Peace,
My Sustainer,
That we may
Endure all,
Tolerate all
In the thought
Of Your grace
And mercy.

Send Your Peace,
My Sustainer,
That our lives may
Become a Divine Vision,
And in Your light
All darkness
May vanish.

Send Your Peace,
My Sustainer,
Our Father
And Mother,
That we,
Your children
On Earth
May all unite
In one family.
Amin.

NAZAR

Sustainer of our
Bodies, hearts and souls,
Bless all that we receive
In gratitude.
Amin.

PRAYER FOR HEALING

You,
Whose nature is
Mercy and Compassion,
Whose being is all peace,
Father, Mother, Creator,
And Sustainer
Of our lives,
Send Your peace on the
Whole of Humanity,
And unite us all
In Your Divine
Harmony.
Amin.

NAYAZ

My beloved Sustainer,
Almighty God!
Through the rays
Of the Sun,
Through the waves
Of the air,
Through the
All-pervading
Life in space,
Purify and quicken me,
I pray; heal my
Body, heart, and soul.
Amin.

Spirit
Of our souls,
Master
Of our minds,
Controller
Of our bodies;
We humbly offer
Ourselves as channels
For Your Love,
Light, and Life,
That we may
Better serve You
And Humanity.
Amin.

Light of all souls,
Life of all beings,
Healer of hearts,
All sufficient,
All powerful God,
Forgiver of our
Shortcomings,
Free us from all
Pain and suffering,
And make us
Your instruments,
That we may,
In our turn,
Free others from
Pain and suffering,
Imparting Your Light,
Your Life, Your Joy
And Your peace.
Amin.

PRAYER FOR THE DEPARTED

You,
Who are the
Cause of the Universe,
The Source from
Whence we come,
And the goal toward
Which we are bound,
Receive the soul of . . .
(say his/her full name here)
Into Your gentle arms.

May Your loving
And merciful
Countenance
Heal his/her spirit,
And remove any burdens
He/she may yet carry.

Surround him/her
With Your warm
And gentle Light,
And elevate him/her
To his/her eternal
Inheritance.

Grant him/her
The blessing
Of Your most exalted
Presence.

May he/she awaken
From the dream
Of this life
Into the glorious vision
Of Your splendor
And sunshine.

We thank You
With all of our hearts
For lending him/her to us
For this short season.

We will treasure
His/her memory
And be grateful
All the days
Of our lives.
Amin.

PRAYER OF HEALING AND BLESSING

My Sustainer,
Heal his/her spirit,
From all the wounds
His/her heart
Has suffered
In this life
Of limitation
Upon the Earth.

Purify his/her heart
With Your Divine Light,
And send Your Mercy
Upon His/her spirit,
Your Compassion
And Your Love.
Amin.

PRAYER FOR THE NEW YEAR

You,
Who abide
In our hearts,
Most Merciful and
Compassionate God,
Sustainer of
Heaven and Earth,
We forgive others
Their trespasses,
And ask Your
Forgiveness
For our own
Shortcomings.

We begin this New Year
With a pure heart
And a clear conscience,
With courage and hope;
Help us to fulfill
The purpose of our lives
Under Your Divine
Guidance.
Amin.

THE UNIVERSAL
WORSHIP SERVICE

INVOCATION

Toward the One,
The Perfection of Love,
Harmony, and Beauty,
The Only Being,
United with all
The Illuminated Souls,
Who form the
Embodiment
Of the Master,
The Spirit of Guidance.

CANDLE LIGHTING

CEREMONY

To the glory of the
Omnipresent Sacred,
We kindle the light
Symbolically
Representing

... the traditions of
Hinduism
... the traditions of
Buddhism
... the traditions of
Zoroastrianism
... the traditions of
Judaism

... the traditions of
Christianity
... the traditions of
Islam

*Additional candles may be
lighted for other traditions
as well, including, but not
limited to:*

... the traditions of
Sikhism
... the traditions of
Taoism
... the traditions of the
Indigenous Peoples

To the glory of the
Omnipresent Sacred,
We kindle the light
Symbolically
Representing
All those who,
Whether known
Or unknown
To the world,
Have held aloft
The light of Truth
Through the darkness
Of ignorance.

33

SAUM

Praise be to You,
God, Most High,
Omnipotent,
Omnipresent,
All-Pervading,
The Only Being.

Take us in Your
Parental arms,
Raise us from the
Denseness of the Earth!

Your beauty
We do worship;
To You we
Willingly surrender.

Merciful and
Compassionate God,
Ideal Sustainer
Of Humanity,
You only
Do we worship,
And toward You alone
Do we aspire!

Open our hearts
Toward Your Beauty;
Illuminate our souls
With Divine Light.

O Perfection of Love,
Harmony and Beauty,
All-powerful Creator,
Sustainer, Judge,
And Forgiver of
Our shortcomings,
Sovereign God
Of the East
And of the West,
Of the Worlds
Above and below,
Of the seen
And unseen beings,
Pour upon us Your
Love and Your Light!

Give sustenance
To our bodies,
Hearts, and souls;
Use us for the purpose
That Your
Wisdom chooses;
Guide us on the path
Of Your Own Goodness!

Draw us closer to You
In every moment
Of our lives,
Until in us is reflected
Your Grace, Your Glory,
Your Wisdom, Your Joy
And Your Peace!
Amin.

READINGS FROM
THE TRADITIONS

We offer to the
Omniscient Sacred
Our reverence,
Our homage,
And our gratitude

... for the light of
Holy Wisdom
(Hinduism)
... for the light of
Sacred Compassion
(Buddhism)
... for the light of
Divine Purity
(Zoroastrianism)
... for the light of the
Holy Covenant
(Judaism)

... for the light of
Divine Sacrifice
(Christianity)
... for the light of
Divine Unity
(Islam)

*Other religious traditions
may be added as well,
including, but not limited to:*

... for the light of
Divine Service
(Sikhism)
... for the light of the
Divine Way
(Taoism)
... for the light of the
Sacred Earth
(Indigenous)

SALAT

Our most
Gracious Sustainer,
Anointing Savior
Of Humanity,
We greet You
With all humility.

You are the First Cause
And the Last Effect,
The Divine Light
And the Spirit of
Guidance,
Alpha and Omega!

Your Light is in all Forms,
Your Love in all Beings:

*Take a moment to imagine
how this is so, as Murshid
suggests . . .*

In a loving mother,
In a kind father,
In an innocent child,
In a helpful friend,
In an inspiring teacher.

*Nor should you limit yourself
to these examples in your
personal prayer.*

Allow us to
Recognize You
In all Your holy
Names and Forms:

*Think of the various
"Names and Forms" by
which God is known in
different religions, and even*

*as embodied in the various
Messengers of those religions
throughout history. These
are some that Murshid
suggests . . .*

As Rama, as Krishna,
As Shiva, as Buddha;
Let us know You as
Abraham, as Solomon,
As Zarathustra, as Moses,
As Jesus, as Muhammad

*If you wish, you may add
others in your personal
prayer.*

And in many other
Names and forms
Known and unknown
To the world!

We adore Your past;
Your Presence deeply
Enlightens our being;
And we look for
Your blessing
In the future!

O Messenger of God!
You, Whose heart
Constantly
Reaches upward,

READING FROM THE WRITINGS OF HAZRAT INAYAT KHAN AND A SERMON

We offer to the
Omniscient Sacred
Our reverence,
Our homage,
And our gratitude
For the light of
Divine Truth.

You come to Earth
With a Message,
As a dove descending
From above
When religion decays,
Speaking the Word
That fills Your mouth,
As light fills the
Crescent Moon.

Let the Star
Of the Divine Light
Shining in Your heart
Be reflected in the hearts
Of Your devotees!

May the Message of God
Reach far and wide!
Illuminating
And making
The whole of Humanity
Into a single Family
In the Parenthood of God!
Amin.

KHATUM

O Perfection of Love,
Harmony, and Beauty,
Sustainer of Heaven
And Earth,
Open our hearts
That we may hear
Your Voice,
Constantly coming
From within.

Disclose to us
Your Divine Light,
Hidden in our souls,
That we may know
And understand life
better.

Merciful and
Compassionate God,
Give us Your great
Goodness;
Teach us Your loving
Forgiveness;
Raise us above
The distinctions
And differences
That divide us.

Send us the Peace
Of Your Divine Spirit,
And unite us all
In Your Perfect Being.
Amin.

BLESSING

May the blessings of God
Rest upon you;
May God's peace
Abide with you;
May God's Presence
Illuminate your hearts,
Now and forevermore.
Amen.

Remembrances

THE TEN
REMEMBRANCES

*A New Version of the
Ten Sufi Thoughts
of Inayat Khan*

I.
There is One God,
The Only Being;
Nothing else exists.

II.
There is one Master,
The Spirit of Guidance,
Constantly leading
Its followers
Toward the Light.

III.
There is one
Holy Writing,
The Sacred
Book of Nature,
The only scripture
That truly enlightens
Its reader.

IV.
There is one Religion,
Unswerving progress
On the true course
Toward the Ideal,
Fulfilling the
Life-purpose
Of every
Soul.

V.
There is one Law,
The Law of Reciprocity,
Observed by a
Selfless conscience
Wedded to a sense of
Awakened justice.

VI.
There is one Family,
The human family,
Uniting the children
Of the Earth,
Indiscriminately
In the Parenthood
Of God.

VII.
There is one Moral,
Love springing from
The transparency
Of the self,
And blooming
In deeds of
Loving-kindness.

VIII.
There is one
Object of Praise,
Beauty that lifts
The heart
Of its worshipper
Through all of its aspects,
Seen and unseen.

IX.
There is one Truth,
The true knowledge
Of our Being,
Within and without;
The essence of all
Wisdom.

X.
There is one Path,
The path of
Making the self
Transparent to the Real,
Raising the limited
Beyond limitation,
The dwelling-place
Of all Perfection.

THE THREE OBJECTIVES

A New Version of the Three Objects of Inayat Khan

I.

To realize and spread
The knowledge of Unity,
The religion of Love
And Wisdom,
So that triumphalism
In religion
May fall away,
The human heart
May overflow with love,
And all hatred caused
By distinctions
And differences
May be rooted out.

II.

To discover
The light and power
Latent in the
Human being,
The secret of all religion,
The power of mysticism,
And the essence
Of philosophy,
Without interfering
With custom or belief.

III.

To bridge
East and West
In thought and ideals,
Forming the
Universal Fellowship,
Where human beings
May meet
Beyond the narrow
Boundaries
Of tribal identity.

THE IRON RULES

My conscientious self:

I.
Make no
False claims.

II.
Speak not
Against others
In their absence.

III.
Do not
Take advantage
Of a person's ignorance.

IV.
Do not boast
Of your good deeds.

V.
Do not claim
That which belongs
To another.

VI.
Do not
Reproach others,
Making them firm
In their faults.

VII.
Do not spare
Yourself in the work
Which you must
accomplish.

VIII.
Render your
Services faithfully
To all who require them.

IX.
Do not
Seek profit
By putting someone
Else in straits.

X.
Harm no one
For your own
Benefit.

THE COPPER RULES

My conscientious self:

I.
Consider your
Responsibility
Sacred.

II.
Be polite
To all.

III.
Do nothing
Which will make
Your conscience
Feel guilty.

IV.
Extend your help
Willingly to those
In need.

V.
Do not look
Down upon
The one who
Looks up to you.

VI.
Judge not
Another by
Your own law.

VII.
Bear no malice
Against your worst
Enemy.

VIII.
Influence no one
To do wrong.

IX.
Be prejudiced
Against no one.

X.
Prove trustworthy
In all your dealings.

THE SILVER RULES

My conscientious self:

I.
Consider duty
As sacred as religion.

II.
Use tact
On all occasions.

III.
Place people rightly
In your estimation.

IV.
Be no more
To anyone
Than you are
Expected to be.

V.
Have regard
For the feelings
Of every soul.

VI.
Do not
Challenge anyone
Who is not your equal.

VII.
Do not
Make a show
Of your generosity.

VIII.
Do not
Ask a favor
Of those who
Will not grant it you.

IX.
Meet your
Shortcomings
With a sword of
Self-respect.

X.
Let not
Your spirit
Be humbled
In adversity.

THE GOLDEN RULES

My conscientious self:

I.
Keep to
Your principles
In prosperity
As well as
Adversity.

II.
Be firm
In your faith
Through all life's
Tests and trials.

III.
Guard the secrets
Of your friends
As your most
Sacred trust.

IV.
Observe constancy
In love.

V.
Break not
Your word of honor,
Whatever may
Befall you.

VI.
Meet the world
With smiles
Through all the
Vicissitudes of life.

VII.
When you
Possess something,
Think of the one
Who does not
Possess it.

VIII.
Uphold your honor
At any cost.

IX.
Hold your ideal high
In all circumstances.

X.
Do not neglect those
Who depend on you.

Notes

Blessing – A blessing composed by Pir-o-Murshid Inayat Khan, traditionally given by cherags at the end of the Universal Worship service.

Copper Rules, the – "The Copper Rules" were composed by Pir-o-Murshid Inayat Khan and are found in the *Vadan*.

Du'a – A prayer of Pir-o-Murshid Inayat Khan found in the *Gayan,* translated and adapted into modern, gender-inclusive English.

Golden Rules, the – "The Golden Rules" were composed by Pir-o-Murshid Inayat Khan and are found in the *Vadan.*

Invocation/Dedication – An invocation composed by Pir-o-Murshid Inayat Khan, adapted here from "the temple of God" to "the temple of the heart," to emphasize going inward at the beginning of one's prayers.

Iron Rules, the – "The Iron Rules" were composed by Pir-o-Murshid Inayat Khan and are found in the *Vadan.*

Khatum – A prayer of Pir-o-Murshid Inayat Khan found in the *Gayan,* translated and adapted into modern, gender-inclusive English. The Arabic word, *khatum,* means 'closing recital.'

Nabi – A prayer of Pir-o-Murshid Inayat Khan found in the Vadan translated and adapted into modern, gender-inclusive English. The Arabic word, nabi, means 'prophet.'

Nayaz – A prayer of Pir-o-Murshid Inayat Khan found in the *Gayan,* translated and adapted into modern, gender-inclusive English. According to Inayat Khan, *nayaz* refers to a kind of "feminine chivalry."

Nazar – A prayer of Pir-o-Murshid Inayat Khan found in the *Gayan,* translated and adapted into modern, gender-inclusive English. The Arabic word, *nazar,* means 'glance' or 'seeing.'

Pir – A prayer of Pir-o-Murshid Inayat Khan found in the *Vadan,* translated and adapted into modern, gender-inclusive English. The Farsi word, pir, means 'elder,' and usually refers to a Sufi master.

Prayer for Healing – A prayer of Pir-o-Murshid Inayat Khan translated and adapted into modern, gender-inclusive English.

Prayer of Healing and Blessing – A prayer of Pir-o-Murshid Inayat Khan translated and adapted into modern, gender-inclusive English.

Prayer for Peace – A prayer of Pir-o-Murshid Inayat Khan translated and adapted into modern, gender-inclusive English.

Prayer for the Departed – A prayer of Pir-o-Murshid Inayat Khan translated and adapted into modern, gender-inclusive English.

Prayer for the New Year – A prayer of Pir-o-Murshid Inayat Khan translated and adapted into modern, gender-inclusive English.

Rasul – A prayer of Pir-o-Murshid Inayat Khan found in the *Vadan,* translated and adapted into modern, gender-inclusive English. The Arabic word, *rasul,* means 'messenger.'

Salat – A prayer of Pir-o-Murshid Inayat Khan found in the *Gayan* translated and adapted into modern, gender-inclusive English. The Arabic word, salat, means 'prayer.'

Saum – A prayer of Pir-o-Murshid Inayat Khan found in

the *Gayan*, translated and adapted into modern, gender-inclusive English. In Farsi, *saum* refers to an 'opening recital,' and in Arabic, to a 'fast' or 'abstention.' Inayati Sufis recite this prayer at dawn, at the beginning of the day (during the fast period), so both the Farsi and Arabic meanings are appropriate. It is also recited at the opening of the formal Inayati gatherings.

Silver Rules, the – "The Silver Rules" were composed by Pir-o-Murshid Inayat Khan and are found in the *Vadan*.

Ten Remembrances, the – These ten remembrances, usually called, Ten Sufi Thoughts, were originally composed by Pir-o-Murshid Hazrat Inayat Khan in 1914 as seven "Sufi Teachings." Later, in 1917, he published a revised list of ten "Sufi Teachings," which, in turn, underwent revisions until 1923, from which time we have the "Ten Sufi Thoughts," as they are used today by most Inayati Sufis. Sharif Graham has suggested that the word "teachings" may still have had too much a flavor of "doctrine" to it, and was thus abandoned in favor of the word, "thoughts." This new version was created to clarify and make the language both gender inclusive and more accessible to modern readers.

Three Objectives, the – The Three Objects were formulated by Pir-o-Murshid Hazrat Inayat Khan and have been translated and adapted into modern English to clarify them and make the language both gender inclusive and more accessible to modern readers.

Toward the One – An invocation composed by Pir-o-Murshid Inayat Khan.

Universel – A prayer of Pir-o-Murshid Inayat Khan translated and adapted into modern, gender-inclusive English. The words "our Temple" were added by his son, Pir Vilayat Inayat-Khan.

HAZRAT INAYAT KHAN

HAZRAT INAYAT KHAN was born in India in 1882. A master of Indian classical music, he gave up a brilliant career as a musician to devote himself full-time to the spiritual path. In 1910, he was sent into the West by his spiritual teacher and began to teach Sufism in the United States, England, and throughout Europe. For a decade and a half he traveled tirelessly, giving lectures and guiding an ever-growing group of Western spiritual seekers. In 1926, he returned to India and died there the following year. Today, his universalist Sufi teachings continue to inspire countless people around the world and his spiritual heirs may be found in every corner of the planet.

Made in the USA
Middletown, DE
19 December 2023